We Love Nature!

We Love Nature!

A KEEPSAKE JOURNAL FOR FAMILIES WHO LOVE TO EXPLORE THE OUTDOORS

STACY TORNIO and KEN KEFFER
Illustrations by DENISE HOLMES

ROOST
BOSTON & LONDON
2014

ROOST BOOKS
An imprint of Shambhala Publications, Inc.
Horticultural Hall
300 Massachusetts Avenue
Boston, Massachusetts 02115
roostbooks.com

9 8 7 6 5 4 3 2 1

First Edition
Printed in the United States of America

♻This edition is printed on acid-free paper that meets the American National Standards Institute z39.48 Standard.
♻This book is printed on 30% postconsumer recycled paper. For more information please visit www.shambhala.com.

Distributed in the United States by Penguin Random House LLC
and in Canada by Random House of Canada Ltd

Designed by Daniel Urban-Brown

LIBRARY OF CONGRESS CATALOGING-IN-PUBLICATION DATA

Tornio, Stacy.
We love nature!: a keepsake journal for families who love to explore the outdoors/Stacy Tornio and Ken Keffer;
Illustrations by Denise Holmes.—First edition.
Pages   cm.
Includes bibliographical references.
ISBN 978-1-61180-101-9 (pbk.: alk. paper)
1. Family recreation. 2. Outdoor recreation. 3. Nature.
4. Diaries—Authorship. I. Keffer, Ken. II. Title.
GV182.8.T67 2014
790.1'91—dc23
2013015906

To the girls who have given me dozens of amazing, priceless, silly, and fun memories over the years—Tina, Ashley, and Amber. —S.T.

To Grandpa & Grandma Keffer and Grandpa & Grandma Ritchie. Thanks for raising eleven nature kids and influencing a whole passel of nature grandkids. —K.C.K.

Contents

Introduction

WE ARE DRAWN TO NATURE from a very young age. Our curiosity leads us to explore our outdoor surroundings. This can mean eating a handful of dirt when we're really little, or hopping on a bicycle and riding off toward the sunset when we're a little older. These innocent moments from childhood can never be recreated exactly, but now with *We Love Nature,* memories can be fully preserved.

We Love Nature is a family book. It's designed for you and your outdoor-loving, fresh-air-seeking kid to complete together. You'll find traditional favorites and things you've maybe never tried before. Think of it as a way to pass along your nature heritage while creating new family traditions. It's equal parts activity guide, nature journal, sketch pad, and keepsake, and there's no right or wrong way to enjoy it. Write in it. Draw in it. Take it with you when you go outside. (Take it with you everywhere!) Fill it up with ideas and sketches inspired by your outdoor adventures when you return home. But above all, experience nature together. It is meant to be shared.

AS AN ACTIVITY GUIDE...

Growing up is about learning new things and applying these skills and ideas as you move forward. *We Love Nature* is structured with this concept in mind. The foundation of the book is fifty-two interactive and unique activities. The activities are arranged with the easier ones first and the more challenging projects later in the book. This doesn't mean you have to start at the beginning, though. They can be done in any order. *We Love Nature* includes a mix of activities suitable for everywhere in nature, from your own backyard to a national park or a wildlife refuge.

AS A NATURE JOURNAL...

Each of the activities includes space to reflect on nature: to jot down memories, to retell your favorite parts of the day, or to plot your next great nature story. We offer a few short creative prompts in every activity to help get you started, but you should always write as much as you want, using extra paper and tucking it between the pages of the book for safekeeping. The prompts and questions will help you collect your thoughts and feelings about being outside. (And maybe they'll inspire you to ask questions we didn't ask!) The more you write, the more you'll remember later.

AS A SKETCH PAD...

For children, one of the best ways to preserve memories is through drawing. There are tons of drawing prompts sprinkled throughout

We Love Nature. Additional blank pages are included at the end of the book, just waiting for your nature kid to be inspired. Maybe some of our illustrations will help inspire you, too. Just like with the writing prompts, use extra paper to capture all your drawings and sketches and fold them inside the book.

AS A KEEPSAKE . . .

We Love Nature will help you preserve those priceless nature moments that you could never capture on video or with a camera. Think of this as an extension of your baby's first keepsake book. The best part is that kids help preserve these memories in their own words and drawings. Cherish sharing nature with your child. After you finish *We Love Nature,* tuck it away in a safe place, along with your other family treasures. Pull it out from time to time to reflect, just like you would a photo album or scrapbook. Or save it for a special occasion when you can pass it along to your nature kid. Before you know it, nature kids will be nature adults, and they can pass on the memories to those they love as well.

The beauty of nature is that it is everywhere. Just open the door—with this book in hand—and step outside.

Meet Our Nature Family

FOR THE KID

Date:

My name:

Nickname:

Age:

What makes me a nature kid?

Why is nature important to me?

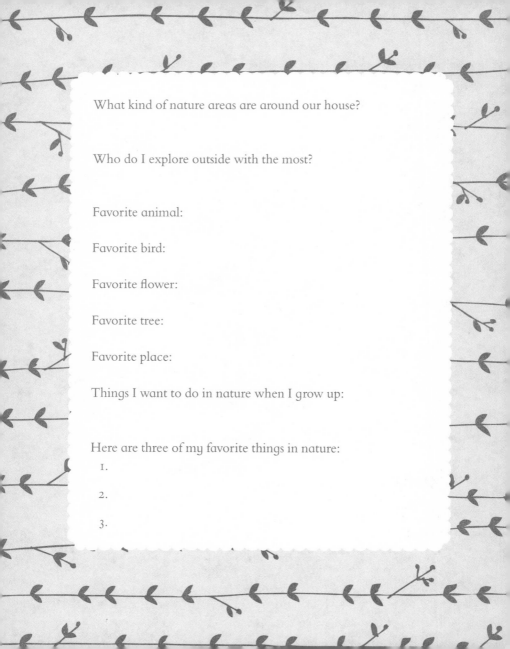

What kind of nature areas are around our house?

Who do I explore outside with the most?

Favorite animal:

Favorite bird:

Favorite flower:

Favorite tree:

Favorite place:

Things I want to do in nature when I grow up:

Here are three of my favorite things in nature:
1.

2.

3.

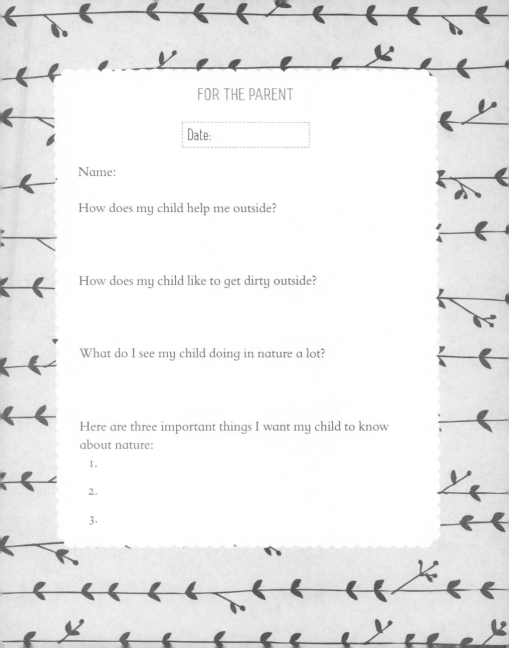

FOR THE PARENT

Date:

Name:

How does my child help me outside?

How does my child like to get dirty outside?

What do I see my child doing in nature a lot?

Here are three important things I want my child to know about nature:

1.

2.

3.

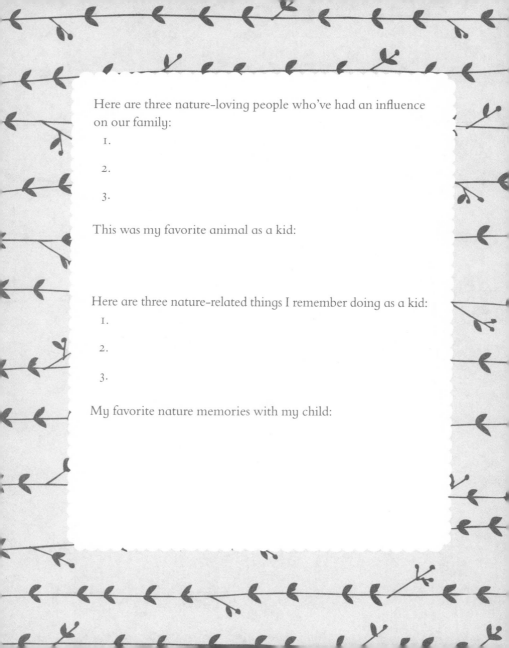

Here are three nature-loving people who've had an influence on our family:

1.

2.

3.

This was my favorite animal as a kid:

Here are three nature-related things I remember doing as a kid:

1.

2.

3.

My favorite nature memories with my child:

THE ACTIVITIES

Sit down, relax, and absorb even the tiniest details around you.

LIFE CAN BE SO HECTIC, it's essential to take an occasional time-out. Pull up a patch of ground or a stump, and plop yourself down. Then—this is the tricky part—stay there for at least 10 minutes. Your first instinct will be to pause for a moment and then immediately go back to what you were doing or move on to what you want to do next. But if you can make yourself stop your activity and remain extra still, you'll see that nature continues on around you. The longer you sit, the more you'll see. Don't just look for bigger, obvious things, either. You might even try getting down on your belly to notice the tiny details that aren't at your normal eye level.

Don't be discouraged if you don't see a lot of action right away. Just taking a time-out for nature is worth the wait!

Predict what you think we'll see in the first minute:

Predict what you think we'll see after 10 minutes:

What did we see within the first minute?

What did we see after the first 10 minutes?

Because we were so quiet, we heard these things:

DIG IN

Bring a notebook with you to take notes while you're sitting still and observing. Soon you'll start noticing even more details like the color of flowers, the height of trees, missing bark where a woodpecker has been pecking, and more.

What did we wish we could see?

If we could choose anywhere in the world to go and observe nature,
where would we go and why?

===== Sketch =====

Choose something besides animals and bugs you saw during your quiet observation
session. Sketch it in its natural surroundings. Make sure everyone in your family gets a
chance to help out with the sketch—someone may have noticed fun details you missed!

Lie back, look up, and invent stories from the shapes in the clouds.

A PERFECT DAY for this is when the clouds are high and puffy in the sky overhead. These fluffy clouds are called cumulus clouds, and they rarely produce rain. You can watch them change shape as they float by. With a little imagination, you'll start to see animals and other shapes in the clouds. With a little luck, you might be able to see an entire zoo of animals in the clouds. Once you see some good clouds drifting by, take turns making up stories about what's happening in the cloud world. The sillier the better with cloud stories, so let your imagination go wild! The best part about this activity is that the results will never be the same twice.

How was the weather on our cloud-watching day?

The first cloud shape we saw was _____.

Sketch our favorite cloud shapes:

The largest cloud shape we saw was _____.

The smallest cloud shape we saw was _____.

When we started looking around elsewhere in nature, what other shapes did we see and where?

_____

Write the story we made up about that cloud:

DIG IN

It's fun to notice the details "hidden" in nature, and clouds aren't the only things that can take on new shapes. Look around your backyard and see if you can find faces, animals, and shapes all around you. For instance, tree bark, flowers, and even sand or grass can all have patterns or shapes that look surprisingly like other things.

Listen to nighttime sounds outdoors, and compare them to daytime sounds.

HAVE YOU EVER NOTICED that when one of your five senses is taken away, the others seem to get amplified? This is certainly the case when it's dark outside and you can't see very well. You end up doing a lot of listening instead. It's easy to be startled by sounds of the night, but they don't have to feel scary! You can hear a lot of cool things after the sun goes down—crickets and other insects, nocturnal animals waking up, and birds settling into trees for the night.

To begin your journey of listening to nighttime sounds, wait for it to get dark. Then bundle up in case it's chilly and head outside with a flashlight. Try not to turn the light on at first, because this will scare away many animals. Instead, explore in the dark as much as you can. Your eyes will adjust to the dark, or you can choose a night when the moon is big and bright. Listen to all the various sounds, and see if you can figure out what each sound is. Once you've listened to sounds at night, try this same exercise during the day. Close your eyes—don't let all the daytime sights distract you. Concentrate on the different sounds around you. What do you hear?

The first sound we heard was _____.

The loudest sound we heard was _____.

While exploring at night, we learned _____.

Listen to sounds outside both at 9 A.M. and 9 P.M. What sounds are
the same and which ones are different?

_____

Try this activity a few months from now. How do the sounds
change from season to season?

_____

What other night sounds can we imagine we are hearing?

_____

DIG IN

Record some of these night sounds. You don't need fancy equipment to do a recording. Most smartphones and computers have the ability to record audio. This will allow you to listen to them again later, so you have a better chance of figuring out the creator of each sound. After listening, try to imitate the sounds you recorded. Who in your family is the best at mimicking the sounds of the night?

What is your favorite nocturnal animal and why?

Play in the mud until you're covered head to toe.

IT'S TIME TO GET MESSY! Instead of worrying about getting muddy and dirty, designate one day to be a "messy day" for the whole family. Give your messy day a special name, and have everyone come up with fun nicknames too. Set aside your grimiest, oldest play clothes, ones you won't mind getting filthy. You can do many things during your messy day. To kick off the day, everyone can put on boots and go out for a walk, trekking through every mud pile and puddle. If it's rained recently and there is plenty of mud, make some mud pies or have a friendly mud toss, throwing globs of mud from one person to another.

If you don't have mud around you, then it's time to make some! Dig up some dirt, dump it in a bucket, and then add water. Mix (with your hands!) until you have a nice mudlike consistency. Then you're ready to make a *real* mess!

We named our messy day _____.

The weather during our messy day was _____.

On this day we did the following:

Other messy activities we came up with:

Our favorite part of messy day was _____ .

Here are the messy nicknames we came up with for each other:

DIG IN

Think about what other fun you can have with mud. You could use it as body paint! You could bury your toes in it and pretend you're at a spa! How about creating a muddy tic-tac-toe board? Build up a smooth mud board, and then use your fingers to take turns making Xs and Os. When the game is over, just wipe it away.

5 Sing campfire songs, and put on a show by the fire.

WHETHER IT IS IN YOUR BACKYARD or at a campground, first things first—you need a campfire. Once you have that taken care of, you need a group of people who aren't afraid to sing. It doesn't matter how good of a singer you are. The crackling of the fire is very forgiving. (If you happen to have someone in the group who can play the guitar, mandolin, or banjo, that's even better!)

Before your campfire sing-along, go online and search for "campfire songs." This will help you discover ones that you might not have heard yet. Plan ahead and print out lyrics to some of these fun songs so everyone can join in.

When you're sitting around the fire, everyone can take a turn picking a song. Sing as many songs as you can before bedtime, and "lights out."

Write the names of the campfire songs we already know:

What new campfire songs did we learn?

Who was the best singer at the campfire and why?

Who loves singing the most and why?

Our favorite part of singing around
the campfire was _____.

DIG IN

Ready to put your singing to the test? Organize a
family talent show around the campfire. Everyone
gets a turn to perform by singing, dancing, telling
jokes, or anything else you can think of.

6 Pet the animals at your county or state fair.

PETTING ZOOS ARE POPULAR destinations for kids of all ages, but another fun, seasonal option is to visit a local fair to see the animals there. (If you don't have a fair near you, you can still visit a farm or a petting zoo and write about your experience here.) At a fair, kids of all ages bring animals they have raised themselves, competing to win awards from judges for "best in show" and other categories. You'll see small animals like chickens and rabbits and larger animals like cows, pigs, goats, and horses. The animal barns are usually open early in the day, and most of the owners don't mind if you stop by to visit. If you go early on in the fair, you might see people grooming and preparing their animals for show. If you go later in the fair, you will see which animals won blue ribbons for first place, red ribbons for second place, and more.

Do we know anyone who raises farm animals?

Which animals do we think we'll see at the fair?

What kinds of animals did we see at the fair?

Which animals were our favorites and why?

What did the animal barn smell like?

Our favorite part of the day was _____.

DIG IN

Find a family farm near where you live and plan a visit to meet the animals. You might even be able to milk a cow, ride a horse, or help gather eggs from the chickens. Are there any dogs and cats at the farm? Are their lives different from the pets you live with?

=== Sketch ===

Use this space to draw your favorite animals of the day. Be sure to label each one and note who drew it.

7 Visit gardens in your town, taking time to stop and smell the flowers.

PUBLIC GARDENS offer some of the finest examples of plants that grow well in your area. Other types of public gardens showcase unique species from all corners of the globe. Whether you're in a formal public garden like a botanical garden or a more casual one like a neighborhood park, you're sure to find a great selection of flora. As a bonus, most public gardens label plants, too, so you can learn the names and some natural history of the flowers. But don't just look at them and read the names. Take a moment to enjoy their beauty and their fragrance.

Find a gorgeous flower, go up to it, close your eyes, and take a deep sniff. Let the scent roll around in your nose for a bit and then breathe it in again. Now go to the next kind of flower and breathe in again. Test the different flowers to figure out which ones smell the strongest. Not everyone likes the same scent, so let each of you smell different flowers to find family favorites.

Where is the garden we visited?

27

Our favorite plants are _____

because _____.

The prettiest plants are _____.

Sketch your favorite plants from gardens you have visited!

DIG IN

Play a game in the garden. Make a list of ten to twenty plants, and then go on a plant hunt to try to find them. Whoever spots them first gets to put their initials down next to the plant's name. Once you've found all the plants or as many as you can on the list, tally up the results on how many plants each person found.

The weirdest plants are _____.

=== Sketch ===

Sketch the weirdest plant you can imagine!

Which public garden would we like to visit next?

Do you have a favorite color? Which flower color has the best scent?

If we made our own flower perfume, we would call it this:

===== Sketch =====

Use this page to sketch a picture of one of the gardens you saw today. Use colored pencils or crayons to make the flowers the right, bright colors, too!

8 Read nature books from the library, and learn something new.

LIBRARIES ARE SOME of the coolest (yet often underutilized) public services available in just about every city and town. If you're lucky, they are within walking or biking distance of your own neighborhood. All libraries have two main sections, fiction and non-fiction. Did you know nonfiction is based on facts, while fiction is based on stories? Today, let's explore nonfiction. Just one shelf in the nonfiction section will open up a whole world of topics to learn about. Not only can you borrow books about specific birds, animals, and trees in your area, but you can also find all kinds of fun books about other aspects of nature, such as baby animals, ways to get dirty, and even animal poop!

Try this: For every two fiction or picture books you borrow at the library, choose a nonfiction book as well. Look through it as a family and talk together about some of the new things you learn. Nature is cool—some of the books will read like storybooks, full of interesting characters and adventures. That's what's so fun about learning!

What new nonfiction subjects do we want to learn about?

Describe the nonfiction section at the library:

Here are some fun books we found:

Now, make a list of the books we checked out:

List three things we learned from one of our books:

1.

2.

3.

Our favorite book was _____

by _____

because _____ .

What subjects do we want to learn about next?

DIG IN

Do a nature-book trivia challenge with your family. Choose a topic, like snakes, whales, or space. Make a list of all the things you already know about these topics. Then find a book or two to check out at the library. Did you learn anything new? What surprised you?

Dance in the rain and stage your very own rain dance.

CAN YOU HEAR RAIN on the roof and splashing in puddles? It's a perfect time for a rain dance! In a downpour or a thunderstorm, you might want to wait until it passes, but otherwise put on your boots and go outdoors! As long as there is no lightning, you can even take an umbrella with you. Instead of standing under it to stay dry, make it a prop in your dance routine.

Dancing in the rain is all about letting go and getting a little (or a lot) wet. Jump through puddles, splash water in wide arcs, throw a little mud around, and just enjoy the feeling of raindrops falling down on your face. The sound of the drops can offer great rhythm, but if you really need some extra tunes to inspire your moves, try playing music through an open window so you can hear it outside. Once you get moving, you'll hardly notice that you're getting drenched.

Describe today's rain dance:

What did we do in the rain besides dance?

How did the rain feel? How wet did we get?

What are we inspired to do outside the next time it rains?

DIG IN

Everyone has tried to catch a snowflake on their tongue. Why not try to catch a raindrop on your tongue? Lean your head back and open up your mouth wide! How many can you catch?

10 Research your state icons, including state bird, tree, and flower.

DID YOU KNOW that every state has not only its own flag but also a long list of state icons? Icons are symbols that represent common or popular things the state is known for. State bird, state tree, and state flower are three of the basics, but there are more state symbols on record than you probably realize. For instance, many states have state mammals, insects, rocks, and more. Some even have a state soil!

Take a few minutes to look up your state's icons online. Are you surprised by what you learned? Write them down and draw them on the next pages, memorize them, and quiz each other. Once

DIG IN

Now that you know all your state icons, are there any states that also share your state bird? What about your state flower? What is unique about your state?

you know a few of your state icons, go outside and explore. See if you can find a few of them in the wild!

Our state bird is:

_____

Our state flower is:

_____

Our state tree is:

_____

Our state motto is:

_____

Which of our state icons have we seen in the wild or at a museum?

_____

What other state symbols do we have and which are our favorites?

_____

Do we have any weird state symbols or icons?

_____

If we were to vote to add a new official state symbol,
what would it be and why?

========== Sketch ==========

Sketch space for your state icons:

Pick the flowers in your garden to make a bouquet (and dry it to make it last year-round).

WHETHER YOU'VE PLANTED a row of vibrant sunflowers or a mix of your favorite native wildflowers, it is nice to bring a bit of this natural beauty into your home. This summer, pick a few flowers from your garden to create your own centerpiece. (If you don't have flowers to pick, see if a friend, neighbor, or family member will allow you to have a few of theirs.) You can gently pick the flowers by hand, or you can use a pair of scissors or garden shears to cut the stems. Cut flowers will need a few inches of stem to drink up the water and stay fresh. Then place the stems in a container of water, such as a vase or a colorful cup, to keep them alive for several days. Changing the water every day or two will help your flower arrangement last longer. Trimming the stem just a little and at an angle when you change the water will help the flowers last, too.

The flowers growing around our yard and area this summer are _____.

Our favorite flowers are _____.

What did we use as a vase for our flower arrangement?

How do our flowers smell?

What flowers do we want to plant next year in our garden?

If we were flowers, here's what we'd look like:

DIG IN

Want to dry your own flowers? It's easy! All you have to do is gather the flowers by the stem and then tie them together with a string. Then hang them upside down by the string in a dry place. You could even hang them in a garage or a basement so nobody touches them. Give the flowers several weeks to dry. Then flip them upright and put them in a vase—no water needed—for a lovely display.

=== Sketch ===

Draw a bouquet of flowers in the space below. Make it the most colorful, crazy bouquet you can imagine. Now you have a bouquet on paper that will last a long time!

12 Gather cool and interesting rocks for your collection.

MUCH OF THE EARTH'S HISTORY is recorded in rocks. Fossils are the best example of this—scientists have learned a lot about the Earth and its prehistoric life based on the fossils and imprints they find. Even if you can't crack the codes of geology yourself, there are some really cool rocks out there for you to discover and collect.

Rocks are surprisingly handy for art and craft projects because they come in just about every shape and size and in many colors. Plus you can write on them, glue things to them, glue them together, use them for mosaics, and more. One easy project is to make a set of checkers from two different kinds of rocks. Instead of red and black checkers, you can use light stones versus dark stones or flat stones versus round stones.

A lot of people like collecting things from places they've visited—these things are called souvenirs—and this is easy to do with rocks. Pick out one special rock from each cool place you visit, and then each one will always remind you of a special memory.

Where did we find the most rocks for our rock collection?

- -

While out on a rock hunt, we found rocks in all these different colors:

- -

===================== Sketch =====================

Sketch our favorite rocks:

Try digging down into the earth a little. We found rocks like this:

What do we plan to do with the rocks we found?

Where would we like to go on a rock-hunting expedition? Why?

DIG IN

Have you ever kept a pet rock? Choose a smooth, shapely rock. With a marker or paints and a paintbrush, draw eyes, ears, and even a tail. The best thing about a pet rock is that you can slip it in your pocket and take it anywhere you want. Go ahead and give it a name, too. Then if you wish, you could create a little rock family or a rock village, using other nature objects like sticks and branches to build streets and houses. What kind of adventures will you and your rocks have together?

Predict the weather, and then track your accuracy.

EVERYONE IS FASCINATED by the weather: What's it going to be like during the day? What does the weekend hold? When is it going to rain again? and so on. Sure, you can always look up the five-day forecast online, but why not take it one step further? Start looking at weather radar maps online, and see how a meteorologist tracks the weather. You'll start to recognize how weather patterns take shape and understand the movement of clouds and weather systems across the country.

After you've read a little more about weather and understand how it works in your particular climate and season, start making your own predictions. Try predicting high and low temperatures, when it's going to rain, how cloudy it will be, and more. The weather is always changing, so no one really knows 100 percent what's in store, but it sure is fun to take a guess!

First, describe the climate of where you live.

Spring: Summer:

Autumn: Winter:

Our weather predictions for the next 5 days are:

NAME	DAY 1	DAY 2	DAY 3	DAY 4	DAY 5

What was the weather actually like the next 5 days?
Draw it in these boxes.

DAY 1	DAY 2	DAY 3	DAY 4	DAY 5

Whose predictions were the most accurate?

======= Sketch =======

What is your ideal weather? Draw a picture here of your very favorite kind of day for playing outside.

DIG IN

Track the weather every day for a month. Two of the best times of year to do this are in spring and fall, because the weather can vary a great deal. Make some predictions along the way. What surprised you the most about the month of weather? Did your predictions come true?

14 Locate a waterfall and capture the beauty with your camera.

WATERFALLS ARE SOME of the most mystical water elements of nature. People travel great distances to see giant waterfalls, but you probably don't have to go that far to find one. Even smaller waterfalls are impressive as you watch the water course over the rocks or plummet over a cliff.

To find the nearest waterfalls, do a little research. Find a list of the waterfalls in your state, and then make a list of the ones you want to visit most. Which one is the closest and which one is the biggest? Then plan a day trip out of your list. Pack a lunch and set out on an adventure to locate three or four waterfalls in one day.

Document your day and take photos of each waterfall you visit so you can remember it. Play with the settings on your camera to create different effects, such as slowing down the shutter speed to create a blur of water, or shooting the waterfall in black and white.

Where are waterfalls near where we live?

Which waterfalls do we want to visit?

Describe our day of scouting waterfalls:

What famous waterfall would we like to see someday?

Our favorite part of our trip
to search for a waterfall was _____ .

DIG IN

Have you ever gone swimming in a waterfall? Try it! It'll probably have to be summer or at least pretty warm weather to do this. Of course, you need to be safe, and wearing a life jacket is a good idea. To start, find a small waterfall and walk through it. What a unique experience!

Now that you've seen spectacular waterfalls in person, get those memories down on paper! Don't just draw the waterfall; draw all the details around it like the rocks, the sky, trees, and everything else you remember.

15 Discover the night sky through stargazing.

ASTRONOMY IS THE STUDY of outer space—the planets, stars, and everything in between—and it is fascinating. An astronomy calendar tells you the phases of the moon, the dates of solar and lunar eclipses, when you can see meteor showers, and so on. Find an astronomy calendar online, and use it to keep track of astronomical events happening in a sky near you. You can also use a star map to help you find constellations in the night sky, which changes throughout the year as the earth moves around the sun.

As you stargaze, make a wish on the first star you see at night. As it gets later and the sky gets darker, you'll see many more stars. Pick a warm night with a cloudless sky, and take along a blanket to lie on and to cover up with after the air cools off. Soon you'll be spotting constellations and, if you are lucky, a shooting star or two.

Starting time of stargazing: _____

Ending time of stargazing: _____

Time we saw the moon: _____

Time we saw the first star: _____

===================== Sketch =====================

Sketch the moon:

Look up the phases of the moon online or in an almanac. What phase was the moon in?

_____

Look up a constellation map online or in a book. Which ones did we find during our stargaze?

When the first star came out, we wished for:

DIG IN

Did you know shooting stars aren't actually stars at all? They are meteors—chunks of rock from space burning up in the Earth's atmosphere. But no one wants to wish on a burning meteor. These "shooting stars" can happen any night of the year, but at certain times there is a predictable increase in meteor activity—this extra action in the night sky is called a meteor shower. Use an astronomy calendar to learn when the next meteor shower will be. And once you've seen one, keep an eye out—maybe you'll get lucky twice in one night!

Invent your own constellations and sketch them here. What are their names?

Swim with your family or friends at a local lake, river, or pond.

ONE OF THE BEST THINGS about swimming is that it's usually free (or very inexpensive), yet it provides hours of healthy entertainment! Some of the best places to swim near you or where you're traveling are probably not crystal-clear swimming pools. Instead, they're natural pools found right outdoors!

Many rivers and lakes are open to the public, and some even have beaches—a great way to enjoy a natural environment. Before you go, pack your swimsuit, a life jacket, towels, sunblock, and even water shoes (the ground can be rocky). You might also take along some water toys like a beach ball to toss around.

Make a list of places nearby we want to go swimming:

Where did we go swimming today?

What water games did we play?

What else did we do around the swimming area?

What parts of nature did we notice while swimming?

Our favorite part of the day was _____.

DIG IN

Don't just take a quick dip on your trip—spend time exploring the shoreline. Walk along the edge of the swimming area to see if you notice any animals. Look at the trees, rocks, and flowers all around. Wherever you find water, there are usually lots of living things around. What new things do you see?

17 Hang up a birdhouse to see which birds you attract to nest.

MAYBE YOU'VE GIVEN your backyard a bird makeover (see page 137), so it's time to add a handcrafted birdhouse to the mix. And why not? A birdhouse will bring personality to your yard, and it could be just the invitation a pair of birds needs to raise their family near your home during spring nesting season.

The types of birds that use birdhouses are called cavity nesters. (Just like a hole in your tooth, a hole in a tree is also called a cavity!) Woodpeckers can create their own cavity by hammering wood with their beaks, but chickadees, wrens, bluebirds, and others are drawn to cavities that already exist . . . or birdhouses you put out!

You can build your own birdhouse if you want. Look for a kit that has everything included—those are fun! If you are feeling ambitious, find plans for building a birdhouse from scratch. Once you have your birdhouse, hang it up in a tree about 6 to 8 feet off the ground. Make sure an adult uses a ladder and hangs the birdhouse up safely.

Don't get discouraged if a bird doesn't show up right away. Sometimes it takes a little while. If you don't get a visitor this spring or summer, leave your house up for birds to roost in at night during fall and winter. Then try again next year. Once you do get a visitor, though, make sure you take time to notice them: what species are they, are they building a nest, and what do they eat?

Where did we get our birdhouse? Did we build it ourselves?

Have we ever found bird nests in our backyard or neighborhood before?

After doing some research online, we learned that the type of birds that will use a birdhouse are _____.

What species of birds do we want to build a house for?

DIG IN

Birds aren't the only critters that will nest in a box. Put up a bat box in your yard, and you might attract another flier into your neighborhood. Bats are neat to watch, and not at all spooky—they flutter around right at sunset as they head out on their nightly insect hunts.

After putting up our birdhouse, what did we notice?

===== Sketch =====

Draw your birdhouse hanging in a tree in your backyard. Don't forget to draw a bird nearby!

Observe wild animals in your area, seeking out their natural habitats.

NATURALIST is a fancy term for someone who studies nature. You can be one, too! Great naturalists don't just casually look at nature. They spend quality time observing it, and they jot down notes and do sketches about the details of nature they witness. This kind of attention to detail takes focus, especially when observing wild animals who rarely sit still while you take in every detail. You have to be patient, and wait for them to come to you.

One way to let wildlife come to you is to use your own backyard if you live in the right kind of setting. Another idea is to go to a park, state forest, or national park to look for animals. Finally, if you don't have any other options, practice your naturalist skills at the zoo. The animals are much more accessible, and you can watch them for hours.

While you're observing, focus on the animals and their environment to study them, watching them interact with other animals if you're lucky, and try to uncover fun details, habits, and more.

Where did we go to observe animals?

What animals did we observe?

Which animal was the funniest and why?

Which animal was the easiest to observe and why?

DIG IN

Animals can act differently in the mornings than later
in the day or just before dark. Observe the differences
in behavior and record them in a journal so you can
compare notes later.

Which animal was the hardest to observe and why?

What was most surprising about the animals we observed?

We discovered the following interesting facts while observing:

===================================== Sketch =====================================

Draw your favorite animals from your trip to the zoo. Try to capture details that other people might not have noticed, like whiskers, spots, or how they walk.

Count the different birds or butterflies in your area.

IF YOU ASK around and do some research, you'll find that there are several national events and programs centered around bird counts. The Christmas Bird Count and the Great Backyard Bird Count are just a couple of the counts you can participate in throughout the year. These are great ways to get outside and pay attention to the different kinds of birds in your area.

A lot of people don't realize that there are butterfly counts, too. Counting butterflies is so much fun, and it's a great way to get a closer look at these beauties. With most counts (birds or butterflies), you tally the different types of birds or butterflies you see. So a monarch butterfly is counted once, even if you see two or three of them flitting about together. You might need a bird or butterfly field guide from your local library to help you identify what you see. It's fun to predict how many butterflies you'll see before the count starts and then see how your numbers stack up when you're done. (Check out the North American Butterfly Association count at naba.org to learn more.)

What kind of count did we do?

Our final number:

How many different types of birds or butterflies did we see?

How many different kinds of birds or butterflies can we identify
without a field guide?

After reading books on birds and butterflies from the library, we
learned a few things like:

Our favorite birds or butterflies are _____ and we

love them because _____.

What was the best part of the day? Why?

Sketch our favorite birds or butterflies:

DIG IN

While most counts only count each species once, you can also try a count where you count everything you see. So if you see four monarchs or four chickadees, you can add eight animals to your day's tally, not two. This is a fun way to keep the day moving a lot faster! If you try this kind of count, you might want to set a time limit or have breaks planned. Get ready to stay busy!

Find inspiration from nature, and then create a piece of art.

MANY ARTISTS HAVE GOTTEN inspiration from nature over the years, and it's not hard to see why. When you're out in the natural world without all the distractions of TV and electronics, your mind is often more open and creative. Ready to try? Go outside to a nature area near where you live—it can be one you're already familiar with or a whole new one. Then start looking around to see what inspires you. Be sure to take a few things with you to help you document what you're seeing. Perhaps it's a sketchbook for sketching or a journal for writing notes. You might also want to take a camera along to capture your favorite things on film.

Inspiration can come from anywhere—up in the trees, down on the ground, or someplace in between. As you're looking around, start thinking about what you want to create. Maybe you can paint something, or perhaps it'll be a collage from your photos. You might even try making nature crafts. Don't limit yourself—let your creativity fly!

Where we went to observe nature:

Here's what we saw that inspired us to create art:

Our favorite part of our adventure was --------------------------------.

Describe the art we created:

DIG IN

Play-Doh is a classic craft material that kids can play with at any age. Try using Play-Doh to create a sculpture from something you saw in nature. Take your time and try to sculpt the little details that you observed, too. Did you know you can make your own Play-Doh? Visit destinationnature.net for our favorite recipe—it's mostly made from salt, flour, and water!

Sketch a few things we noticed:

Did we find other nature art ideas online or in books?

What kind of art do we want to create next?

21 Jump into piles of autumn leaves.

THE MOST IMPORTANT PART of jumping into an autumn leaf pile is to first build a *really huge* pile. If there are enough leaves on the ground, you can create an obstacle course of sorts with leaves outlining a path and a big pile at the end. Don't have a big yard or leaves to rake? No worries! Ask neighbors, family, or friends if you can rake in their yard. You might even head to the park to rake up a pile there.

You're going to need one rake per person for this, and a tarp might come in handy, too. Get everyone involved—rake up leaves onto a tarp and then drag them into one central area. If you can pile them at the bottom of a slide, off the side of a small deck, or at the bottom of a hill, you'll have a "runway" for picking up speed. Really take the time to build up a huge pile. This way, you'll be able to jump in it many more times before you have to rebuild it. Once it's as huge as you can make it, take turns jumping or sliding into it. Be sure to go one at a time so you don't bonk heads!

Describe the weather on our leaf day:

Where did we build our leaf pile?

How long did it take us?

We measured our leaf pile, and this is how wide it was:

DIG IN

Turn your leaf pile into a treasure hunt. Get little animal figurines or other objects and hide them among the leaves. Then start a timer and see who can find the hidden treasures the fastest.

And this is how tall it was:

What else can we do with the leaves besides jump into them?

===================================== Sketch =====================================

Sketch a picture of our favorite leaf shapes from our pile:

Our favorite part of building

a leaf pile is _____.

Sled down the biggest hill around, testing out different sledding styles.

YOU'RE GOING TO NEED a big pile of snow and a good hill to go sledding, but it's well worth the wait for winter! Sledding on a sled or tube is something almost everyone can do, since you don't need to have any skills other than sitting. The best time to go sledding is right after a snowfall. This way, the snow is fresh and fluffy, and every run you take will help pack the snow into the hill, creating a smooth run. If you live in an area that gets plenty of snow in the winter, you will just need patience for a favorable forecast and a little sleuthing to find the best, safest sledding hill (avoid trees or other obstacles). If there's no snow where you live, see if there are ski areas nearby that offer snow tubing for families. Or maybe you can plan to try sledding on your next cold-weather family vacation. Don't forget to take gloves, a hat, warm clothing, water-resistant layers, snow boots, and maybe even goggles so you can still see when you are zooming down the hill.

Where we went sledding:

The gear and supplies we took sledding:

A funny story about our day of sledding:

DIG IN

After you get a feel for the sledding hill, experiment
for some added thrills. Go down the hill on your belly,
go sideways, link your tubes together by holding on
to one another's handles. Be creative, yet resourceful!
Just don't forget to take a hot cocoa break in between
runs to stay warm.

Our favorite part of sledding is _____.

Sketch the sledding hill:

23. Design your yard and garden to be butterfly friendly.

YOU MAKE YOUR YARD BIRD friendly by offering food, water, and shelter, but what do you do to bring in the butterflies? The best way is to have a butterfly-friendly garden. You can do this in two ways—first by having nectar plants and second by having host plants. The good news is that almost all plants have a nectar source, so you can't really go wrong with any flowers. Butterflies seem to especially like purple flowers, so consider planting veronica, petunias, and catmint.

Host plants are unique to each kind of butterfly—they are plants that butterflies lay their eggs on, so that their caterpillars can feed on the plant when they hatch. Butterflies need very specific host plants for their caterpillars: you can plant milkweed for monarchs or dill for the black swallowtail, for instance. For more host plant or nectar ideas, check out a butterfly gardening book at your local library.

The type of butterflies we want to attract is _____.

How did we make our yard more butterfly friendly?

_____

The nectar plants we planted are _____.

The host plants we added are _____.

After reading a butterfly gardening book, here's what we learned:

_____

DIG IN

Want to try another way to bring in butterflies to your yard? Put out a butterfly feeder. Butterfly feeders will have a reservoir either for sugar water or for fruit. And get this—butterflies like older or even rotting fruit. So when the fruit in the kitchen starts to spoil, put it out for the butterflies!

What plants do we want to add to our butterfly garden next? Sketch them here:

Build castles in the sand, and create other beach art.

IF YOU LIVE NEAR THE OCEAN, building sand castles might be standard summer fare for you. But you don't necessarily have to live near the ocean to play in the sand. Lots of lakes, rivers, and even small ponds have a beach area you can go to as well.

Go ahead and plan a whole day around it—pack a picnic lunch along with other beach essentials like sunblock, towels, a bucket, shovels, and other sand toys.

The best type of sand for building castles and other sculptures is slightly damp. The dry top layer of sand won't work well for your building. Instead, dig down a little bit and get the darker sand—it is perfect for packing, shaping, and sculpting. Once you have mastered building sand castles, move on to creating little people, animals, and other items. Create a whole village!

Where we had our beach day:

What was the weather like on our beach day?

Who came with us?

What did we each bring?

DIG IN

Have you ever buried yourself in the sand? You can bury your whole body, or just cover your feet, arms, or legs. Or take turns burying one another in the sand. Don't forget to take pictures!

Describe how the sand felt:

=============================== Sketch ===============================

What did we build in the sand? Draw it here:

25 Cook s'mores over an open campfire.

CAMPING isn't camping without a little cooking over an open fire. Hot dogs are a great campfire food to cook on a stick, followed by the perfect dessert: ooey, gooey s'mores. Grab your marshmallows, chocolate, and graham crackers and circle up around the fire.

Roasting the perfect marshmallow takes practice. Some people like to cook them fast, even though the marshmallows can get a little charred. Others like to roast them slowly and steadily so they warm up all the way through. No matter how you do it, make sure you have a cooking stick that is long enough so you don't have to stand too close to the fire. Once your marshmallow is ready, sandwich it with a piece of chocolate between two graham crackers. Squish it all together and eat it up!

Where did we have a campfire?

What is our favorite ingredient in the s'mores?

How do we like our marshmallows roasted?

Who roasts the best marshmallows?

The best part of making s'mores is _____.

DIG IN

When you cook over open fire, you're cooking like humans have done for thousands of years. It's how *everyone* used to cook. What else can you cook on a stick over a fire besides hot dogs and marshmallows? Try wrapping sliced turkey and cheese around a stick and cook that. What about a slice of bread slathered in peanut butter and rolled up? Experiment with familiar foods in different forms to see what you like most.

Map your own nature tour.

MAPS HAVE ALWAYS BEEN an essential part of our lives because they help us navigate a complex world and get us where we want to go. Even though a lot of people just use online maps these days, it's worth the effort to take out a paper map and study it.

Each map is designed a little differently, but all have similar features. Look for the compass pointing out north, south, east, and west. All maps will also have a scale telling you how to calculate distance; 1 inch on a map might equal 1 mile or it might be 1,000 miles.

Maps can also help us discover places in nature that we might not ever find on our own! Use existing maps to create your own trip map, marking five different parks you'd like to explore near your home. Then get going and start exploring!

How close to you is the closest park?

Which park is the farthest away?

How will you get to each of your destinations?

======================= Sketch =======================

Make and illustrate your very own memory map. Draw something special here from
each park you visited. Number them from 1 to 5, based on the order you visited them. If
you want, add labels or captions to each drawing. Then draw a road from one drawing
to the next, in order, to recreate your trip. It does not have to be an accurate road map!

DIG IN

What are other places or locations on a map you could plan a tour around? How about gardens or ponds? Find other natural features that you want to explore. If you really challenge yourself to investigate it, you'll quickly learn that nature is everywhere. You can connect with nature anywhere you go.

Name where you went and describe your visits!

Park #1:

Park #2:

Park #3:

Park #4:

Park #5:

Our favorite park was _____.

because _____.

27 Experiment with starting seeds, both veggies and flowers.

WHEN THE WEATHER OUTSIDE is chilly, blustery, or snowy, it's a good time to daydream about gardening. It's fairly easy to start seeds indoors. Plus, this provides a great opportunity for kids to really see firsthand how the process works.

If you don't have seeds already, hit your local garden center. Many have a great seed selection year-round, and it's fun to go through the aisles to browse and plan. You'll need just a few supplies: seeds, soil mix, and a container of some sort. Once you're home, it's time to plant. Follow the guidelines on the back of the seed pack as to how deep to plant the seeds. You can either plant them in a biodegradable pod you buy at the gardening center or be creative and plant seeds in a recycled object, such as a clean yogurt container or even an old Easter or Halloween bucket. (Just make sure the bottom has drainage holes.) Some seeds will sprout within a day or two, while others might take a week or more. Be sure to offer the seeds plenty of sunshine and take care not to overwater them. Then, when the seed turns into a sprout, transfer the sprouts outside into the ground.

While this project is best to do when it's nice out, you could modify it in cooler temperatures by planting herb seeds and just keeping the pots indoors. Be sure you provide plenty of light—seedlings need a lot of fuel.

Seeds we want to start and why:

DIG IN

You often see big flats (sometimes twenty or more flowers) at the garden centers, and they even have the supplies to grow your own. Try starting a whole flat of flower seeds—good options include marigolds, sunflowers, and zinnias. Then move them outside and nurse them carefully. It's very rewarding to grow something from seed all the way through flower!

How long did it take the seeds to sprout?

Draw the seeds here:

Draw the sprouts here:

When did we transfer the seeds outside?

What other plants do we want to grow from seed?

================ Sketch ================

What fruits, vegetables, or flowers are growing from our seedlings? Draw them here:

Shop for fresh food at your local farmers' market to make a meal.

A VISIT TO the farmers' market is always an adventure, so grab your reusable bags and check it out. There are so many options, it's like a scavenger hunt for the best produce and other fun foods. Farmers' markets reinforce the seasonal nature of food harvests. From early-season specialties like strawberries and asparagus to late-fall squash and sweet potatoes, the flavors and smells are more intense at the farmers' market than at the grocery store. You'll never be disappointed when you eat a meal made from farm-fresh produce.

Find the nearest farmers' market, and note the days of the week it is open. Visit multiple stands. Getting to know the farmers at the market is a key part of the experience. They are always happy to answer questions about their produce and their farm, and they may even offer samples. If you're stumped about what to make for a meal, they can give you tips about new recipes. If there are picky eaters in the family, let them choose some produce themselves for tonight's dinner. Then let everyone help prepare the meal, and enjoy a fresh taste of some local produce as a family!

Our favorite part of the farmers' market is _____.

What did we see the most of?
_____

Did we discover any produce or food that we'd never seen before?
What was it?
_____

DIG IN

Go to a farm where you can pick your own produce.
This is especially common with strawberries in spring
and apples in fall, but you can find other veggies to
pick if you look around and do some research. These
are great ways to get a sense of what it feels like to
work on a farm.

How many vendors did we visit? _____

What were their names and where are their farms?

_____

Our shopping list:

_____

What recipe are we making?

_____

29 Carve a pumpkin, and then roast the seeds.

IT ISN'T AUTUMN without carving pumpkins! It's a slippery, slimy, messy, delightful activity, so lay down some newspaper on your countertop or table before you begin or just carve it outside. If you have a garden, start early by planting pumpkin seeds in early summer. If you missed out or don't have space, go to a pumpkin farm instead. It's great to be out on a farm and in nature, selecting your favorite pumpkin from the field. (If you can't get to a farm, there are pumpkins at the grocery store, too!)

Once you have selected your own pumpkin, get help from a grown-up to slice the top, cutting at an angle, to make your lid. Scoop out the insides and scrape all the stringy flesh off the sides of the pumpkin. See all the seeds? Be sure to save as many seeds as you can for roasting (or for planting next summer). Then you just need to carve your jack-o'-lantern's face. Here's another idea—try carving a nature design instead. You can use a pattern or go freestyle to try motifs like an owl, spider, leaf, flower, or tree.

How did we each choose our pumpkins?

What else did we see while at the pumpkin farm?

Describe everyone's pumpkin and how they carved it:

DIG IN

Try growing your own pumpkin from seed. It's best
to start your seeds outside in June or July so you have
pumpkins in time for Halloween. When you have
a tiny pumpkin growing on the vine, here's a neat
trick—carve your name into the skin of the pumpkin.
This scar will remain on the pumpkin as it grows, and
you'll always know which pumpkin belongs to each
person in the family.

Who carved the scariest pumpkin? _____.

The most creative pumpkin? _____.

Describe what the insides of the pumpkin felt like:
_____

Our favorite part of carving pumpkins is _____.

===================== Sketch =====================

Sketch out a few jack-o'-lantern designs for your pumpkin carving. Remember simple
shapes are the easiest to carve out. You can mix and match circles, triangles, diamonds,
and other shapes into many fun faces.

Hike on the trails near your home, and write about what you discover.

HIKING DOESN'T take any special equipment, and anyone can do it—you're simply going for a walk in nature, and it's a blast! Hiking is a great activity for a day trip, and exploring area trails is a top thing to do while you're on vacation. No matter where you go hiking, be sure to pack plenty of water and a few trail snacks. You'll probably be gone a lot longer, go a lot farther, and get a lot more exercise than you'd think! When you first get to the trailhead, you may be excited to get going right away. But don't take off hiking as fast as you can—you need to conserve your energy. Slow and steady is the best way to experience nature, and it's the best way to hike, too. While you're moving along, stop for plenty of breaks along the trail. When you pause, take in the scenery around you, and if you find an especially lovely spot, take a photograph or sketch the scene in the space provided in this section.

Where we hiked:

Length of trail:

How long it took us:

The weather for our hike was _____.

How was nature different on the trail than in our backyard?

The next trail we would like to hike on is _____.

DIG IN

Oftentimes, hiking trails have both easy and hard paths. Once you get to a point where you can do an easy hike pretty well, go ahead and try a hard one, even if it's only for a little section. Compare it with the easy one. What made the harder path more challenging?

What did we see on the trail?

Our favorite part of hiking was _____.

================= Sketch =================

Every trail is a bit different. Draw a picture of your favorite trail, and try to add as many details as you can. It would be fun to even draw your family in the picture as you're hiking along the trail.

Reuse an object as a garden container, filling it with potting soil and plants.

CONTAINER GARDENING is popular because it doesn't take up much space—you just need a small spot on a stoop, corner of the deck, or even a patio. You don't even need to buy new pots—people have turned just about everything imaginable into a home for plants, including worn-out boots, old coffee cups, and even a charcoal grill. It's cool to give an object a whole new, unique purpose. Reusing objects is good for the planet, too, because it keeps things out of the landfill.

If you're looking for inspiration for a container garden, first check out what's in your house that you can repurpose. If you can't find anything, go to a local rummage sale, yard sale, or thrift shop and see what clever containers you can find for less than a dollar. Just be sure you can drill drainage holes into the bottom of your object—things made of metal, stone, or other super-hard materials might be super-hard to drill!

Very important: Don't forget to water your plants every 2 or 3 days so they thrive.

What do we have in the house that would make good garden containers?

Do a little research together online. What are some fun garden containers other people have created?

After a trip to a rummage sale or thrift store, what items did we see that would work as containers?

DIG IN

How do you know what plants to place in which containers? Look to the experts. When you are at the garden center, look at what they put in their containers. Maybe you have a friend or neighbor who gardens and who has some good ideas for you! As you select plants, read the label to learn things like whether they require sun or shade, so you can take care of them properly. And don't forget to water them! The soil in pots and containers dries out very quickly in the sun.

What plants or types of plants do we want to grow in our container? Are they edible?

What was our favorite part of planting the garden?

What do we want to plant next time?

============================ Sketch ============================

Sketch of our container garden here:

Travel to a national wildlife refuge or national park, and discover new animals or landscapes.

32

NATIONAL WILDLIFE REFUGES and national parks are areas that have been set aside for the general public to enjoy. Lucky for you, they also provide outstanding opportunities for people to explore the outdoors. Plus, they are generally free or have very low fees.

First, you need to find a refuge or a park. You can do this online at refuges.fws.gov or at nps.gov. All you have to do is enter your state! Chances are, there's already a refuge or park within a one- or two-hour drive. Once you find an area you want to visit, look to see if it has any upcoming events or educational programming. Many have hiking trails or places to bike, and several even have special family programs. You might want to plan your day a little ahead of time to make the most of it. Look up all the activities you can do, and take a family vote. Then get outside and experience these great nature areas for yourself.

List of state refuges and parks:

Which places do we most want to visit?

What activities or events are at the places we're going to?

What does everyone want to do most?

What do we need to bring with us?

Describe our day at the park:

What animals or nature elements did we see?

Our favorite part of the refuge or park was _____.

What do we want to do at our next visit?

_____

DIG IN

What if you could turn your favorite place into a protected natural park? What would you name it, and what would your logo be? Draw it here.

Sketch

Write a nature story after a nature hike or outdoor journey.

WRITING IS ONE of the best ways to preserve a memory, and it's also a great tool for documenting the natural world around you. Try taking notes about things you observe while on a hike or on a walk through your local park, and then turn it into a story. Every good story needs a few basic components—people (characters), places (setting) for people to go, and things (objects) for people to interact with. Every good story also needs action (plot)—what happens to the people, when, and where?

When you get back from your walk, take a look at the notes you jotted down. Go over your ideas with your family and start a conversation about how you want to craft your nature story. (Use extra paper or type it up if you need more room to write!) Be sure to put it in a safe place so you can preserve it for years to come.

Setting: Where did we go on our hike or walk? What was the landscape like? What kind of day was it? What was the weather?

Characters: Who did we see? What animals did we see?

Objects: What interesting or unique things did we see along the way?

Plot: What happened to us along the way? What happens to the people or animals in the story we are writing?

Now, write the story!
Use all the space here or add extra sheets of paper.

34

Collect treasures outdoors to turn into a nature collage.

NATURE CAN INSPIRE the artist in everyone! One of the easiest ways to create a piece of art is through collage—plus it's a great project to work on as a family. Creating a masterpiece is as easy as taking a walk in your backyard and gathering up natural objects like twigs, leaves, or flowers. Even the smallest items from nature, like pinecone petals, pieces of bark, and seedpods, will add that perfect touch of detail. Then, all you need is poster board, foam board, or wood to use as a background, and some glue for securing everything together on the background.

You'll want to lay out your design first, before gluing down all your treasures. What shapes can you make with the bits and pieces from nature you gathered? Be creative when making your collage—leaves are some of the most versatile things to use, because you can shape them into people, animals, or clouds. When you're done, sign your name and write the date on your piece of art so you can preserve the memory.

What we found in the backyard for a collage:

What we found in the backyard that wouldn't work:

===== Sketch =====

Sketch a design for your collage before you even go for a nature walk. How do you want it to look when it's done? What are all the different items you'd like to use? Now look for objects in nature that will help achieve the design.

If we lived near the ocean, what objects would we find for a collage? What if we lived near the mountains?

Our favorite collage object was _____
because _____.

Write a story about what's happening in our collage:

DIG IN

Frame your picture with objects from nature, too. Small branches make great picture frames, as do pinecone petals and tiny colorful stones. Using glue, put your border into place, one item at a time. Give it lots of drying time, and add more glue as needed so everything will stay in place.

Invite your friends over to play some outdoor games.

SIMPLY BEING OUTSIDE is the gateway to an appreciation for nature. You don't need to be in the woods or at a nature center to make the most of being outside. Get out there and appreciate the outdoors by playing games either in your backyard or at a local park. It's a lot more fun to play games when you have a big group together, so the more the merrier! This is perfect for a family reunion or a neighborhood block party. You could even have fun and call it the Neighborhood Olympics or the Family Playoffs.

When everyone arrives, have each person write down the name of a game he or she wants to play on a piece of paper. The game shouldn't require a lot of supplies—games like tag and hide-and-seek are perfect! Once everyone has written down a game, fold up the pieces of paper and put them all in a hat. Take turns drawing out a slip of paper, announce the game to the group, and spend at least 15 minutes playing this game. Then move on to the next one. It doesn't matter how many people you have over or how young or old they are, it'll be fun to try a slew of new games.

Who did we invite over?

The games people suggested playing were _____.

Some of our favorite games were _____.

Who won?

_____

Sketch all the people who played games:

What are the rules of our favorite game?

The best part of the day was ------------------------.

UP, UP, and AWAY!

DIG IN

A bag of balloons can add a ton of lively fun to any backyard gathering. There are so many ways you can use them. You can play "tennis" by batting an inflated balloon back and forth with racquets.

Here's one more fun idea for a backyard game: let's call it Up, Up, and Away! First, give everyone a balloon to inflate. Then have each person toss his balloon up in the air. Everyone must keep the balloon in the air by hitting it skyward with an arm, head, back, or any other part that reaches it. The last person to keep his balloon in the air without it touching the ground wins! Make sure to keep nature clean by disposing of the balloons when you're done.

Learn different birdsongs, and then test your memory.

A LOT OF PEOPLE can recognize a bird just by hearing its song. It's a pretty handy skill. For instance, if you know what a cardinal sounds like, when you hear it you know where to look to find it. Set a family goal to learn the songs of birds common to your area, starting with ten or twelve. It's a good idea to pick ones that you're familiar with, so you have a chance of hearing them and exercising your knowledge. Then research birdsongs online to find recordings. Listen to them several times, and then quiz each other by playing them one at a time and making people recall which one is which. Once you learn them really well, test out your skills around your backyard and neighborhood. Maybe one day you'll hear an answer from high up in the trees!

Birds whose songs we want to learn:

Birds we see in our backyard or around the neighborhood:

- -

Describe the birdsong we hear most often
and spell out the "words" to the song:

- -

Our favorite birdsong is -

because - .

DIG IN

Go beyond birdsongs. What other natural noises are
in the backyard? If you listen closely, you can probably hear squirrels scurrying up the trees and bugs
rustling through the grass. Once you start learning
how to appreciate nature through sounds, the whole
world opens up.

Which other birdsongs do we want to learn?

===== Sketch =====

It's tricky to figure out which birds go with which songs. Draw a picture of two or three of your favorite birds. Then under each one, spell out the words of their songs. Are any birds named after their songs?

Create a scavenger hunt in your backyard.

YOU CAN SPEND EVERY DAY playing in your backyard and think you know it pretty well, but a scavenger hunt challenges you to see things in a new light. You can create scavenger hunts a few different ways. Try making a list of things to find based on simple descriptions—something orange, something round, something soft, and so on. Use your imagination to make the list as long as you'd like. Then you can take turns or work together to find all the objects that fall into the specific categories. You can also work in teams, depending on how many people are playing. Each team uses the same scavenger hunt list. The first team to find all the items on the list wins.

Another way to do a scavenger hunt is by making it a photo hunt. This means whoever is looking for the item has to take a digital photo of it when he or she finds it. At the end, everyone has fun going through the photos to talk about what was found.

What kind of scavenger hunt did we plan?

Who participated?

Name ---------------------- Favorite part of the hunt:

Name ---------------------- Favorite part of the hunt:

Name ---------------------- Favorite part of the hunt:

What did we find that was round?

What did we find that was orange?

What did we find that was soft?

Add your own adjectives and scavenger hunt items to the list:

What did we find that was _____?

What did we find that was _____?

What did we find that was _____?

What did we find that was _____?

What did we notice in the backyard that we'd never noticed before?

_____

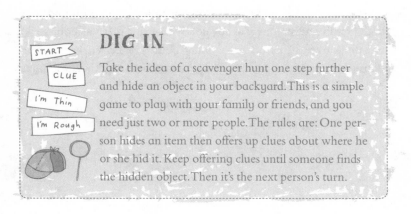

DIG IN

Take the idea of a scavenger hunt one step further and hide an object in your backyard. This is a simple game to play with your family or friends, and you need just two or more people. The rules are: One person hides an item then offers up clues about where he or she hid it. Keep offering clues until someone finds the hidden object. Then it's the next person's turn.

Pack a lunch, camera, and journal for an outdoor picnic.

GOING ON A PICNIC is one of the greatest outdoor family pastimes. You wake up in the morning, pack up a lunch, a camera, and a journal to record your day, and then off you go! It doesn't matter where you're going—swimming, hiking, or just to the local park—the picnic itself is the event! Let everyone be involved in packing up the picnic lunch and choosing the food.

Once you're done eating, don't just pack up and leave your picnic site. Take some time to relax and explore the area around you. Take pictures, write down what you see, or just take off your socks and shoes to feel the soft grass under your feet. Let each person in your family pick one activity that everyone does together. It'll make the whole day even more memorable.

We packed for our picnic the following meal:

Where we went for our picnic:

To make our picnic special, we took along ------------------------------.

What did we see around our picnic site?

What was our favorite activity? Whose idea was it?

================================== Sketch ==================================

A sketch of our picnic site:

DIG IN

You can play a simple word game called "I'm Going on a Picnic." To play, someone starts by saying, "I'm going on a picnic, and I'm going to bring an apple," or anything that starts with the letter A. Then, the next person thinks of something that starts with a B that he or she will bring. Go through the whole alphabet naming items (both serious and funny) that you'd bring to a picnic. You can make it themed—food, animals, people—or keep it general.

Our favorite part of the picnic was:

For our next picnic we want to go to:

Bike beyond your backyard to see a whole new side of nature.

WITH OR WITHOUT training wheels, biking is fun and great exercise at any age. Adults can even tow youngsters in a bike trailer until they are ready for their own set of wheels. For older kids, biking opens up the entire neighborhood for these young explorers. Many communities have bike trails or paths around parks that keep riders away from roads and traffic. A short bike ride is great exercise, and you can't beat the rush of wind blowing over your face and through your helmet. You might even find biking so enjoyable you'll decide to just leave the car at home on your next trip to the grocery store or when you go visit friends down the street.

Another bonus of traveling by bike is that it lets you experience direct contact with nature. You can hear the birds sing as you ride by, you can experience the weather firsthand, and you can discover hidden treasures you wouldn't be able to get to by car. What else makes biking special?

Our favorite place to bike is _____.

We like biking because _____.

Who likes biking the most in the family?
_____

Name one thing in nature we observed while on a bike ride:
_____

DIG IN

Turn your bike ride into an adventure hunt, picking
up treasures wherever your travels take you. To do
this, you'll want to have a basket secured on your bike
or a backpack you can wear comfortably as it fills up
with your special finds.

If we could bike anywhere in the world, where would we go?
(Don't worry about crossing oceans or mountains!)

Imagine our bikes have names. What are they?

On one bike outing, here's a funny thing that happened:

Search for tracks and other signs of animals in the woods.

HAVE YOU EVER seen a mysterious set of footprints in fresh snow or in the mud? It's fun to find tracks outside and do some sleuthing to figure out which animals they belong to. It's almost like a puzzle; each little footprint detail is like a clue. The best time to look for tracks is a day or two after a rain. This is because the ground is softer and easier for feet to make imprints.

If you want pictures of animal tracks to use as a reference out in the field, check out a book from the library. You could also take a camera along and photograph the tracks you find. Then when you come home you can do research online to figure out what you saw. Pretty soon, once you are familiar with animals in your area, you'll be able to recognize their tracks on your own.

Where did we go to look for animal tracks?

126

What other details did we notice near the tracks?

From books and websites about tracks, we learned _____.

============================ Sketch ============================

What kind of tracks did we find? Sketch them here:

deer

fox

wild turkey

DIG IN

Once you've mastered tracking, it's time to look for animal scat. What is scat? *Scat* is just another word for poop. Believe it or not, there are books devoted to animal poop, so you can learn how some poop looks different from other poop. Keep an eye out for animal poop in the woods, and use the same tools you used for tracking to figure out what animal it came from!

41 Photograph your adventure while visiting a nature center.

FROM BROAD LANDSCAPES to close-up flowers, there are all kinds of beautiful things to photograph everywhere you look outdoors. Digital photography makes it wonderfully easy to turn kids loose to take as many photos as they please; plus it's fascinating to see the world through their eyes.

For a fun challenge, go to a nature center and pretend you're on a safari photo shoot. After you return home you can have plenty of fun creating a scrapbook of your nature adventure. Print out your favorite shots from the day and label them with captions. Jot down highlights here or in a journal, so you'll remember what you saw when you look back.

Here's one great tip for taking nature photos—no matter what you are photographing, the light will be best at dawn and dusk. Sunlight in the middle of the day is too harsh. As a bonus, you'll have a better chance of spotting wildlife around sunrise and sunset, too, when they tend to be more active.

When you are exploring outdoors, what are
your favorite things to take pictures of?

What are the easiest things in nature to take pictures of? Why?
What are the hardest?

Describe our photo shoot day:

The best photo of the day was of _____.

Can you think of funny nature photos you'd like to take?

Our dream subject for a photo is _____.

DIG IN

Enter your wildlife photograph in a contest! You can find all kinds of national and local contests to submit to. You could even enter it in the county fair for the chance to win a blue ribbon!

Paddle a kayak or canoe along a lazy river or lake.

PADDLING ALONG a river or across a lake is a great family activity that everyone can be a part of. Even the youngest explorers can come along for the ride—everyone just needs to wear a life vest.

Most kayaks are built for one person, but many stores and rental places offer tandem kayaks, too. Kayaks can be tricky to get in and out of unless you have a sit-on-top style, like a sea kayak. Canoes are more stable, and they hold more people, too, so they are a great option for a family paddle or for beginners.

If you have your own canoes or kayaks, just load them on the car before driving to your paddling destination. Otherwise you can easily find a place to rent them near a body of water. If you have an explorer who is big and strong enough to paddle on his own, be sure to let the canoe or kayak renters know. They might have smaller-size boats for kids who can go on their own safely. Make sure life jackets are available that fit all your paddlers, too.

Don't forget to take in all of nature while you're cruising through the water—keep your eyes open for birds, beavers, turtles, fish, and other aquatic plants and animals.

We went canoeing / kayaking (circle one) with:

Where did we go?

How long did we paddle for?

Here is a list of the animals we saw during our trip:

What kinds of trees and other natural things
did we see during our trip?

The easiest part of our paddling trip was‗‗‗‗‗‗‗‗‗‗‗‗‗‗‗‗‗‗

and the hardest part of the trip was‗‗‗‗‗‗‗‗‗‗‗‗‗‗‗‗.

Our favorite part of the trip was‗‗‗‗‗‗‗‗‗‗‗‗‗‗‗.

DIG IN

Once you have a good handle on canoeing or kayaking, set some paddling goals. Maybe you want to paddle for half an hour before taking a break. Or maybe you can boat out to a specific destination, such as an island or a rope swing! Set a goal as a family, and you'll all share a great sense of accomplishment when you complete it.

43 Savor the ultimate snow day—make snowmen, snow angels, and more.

CELEBRATE SNOW together by having the ultimate snow day. After a fresh snowfall, brainstorm all the things you could do in the snow, and then go out to experience them. Here are a few ideas to get you started: make snow ice cream, build a snowman, play snow tag, make snow angels, build a bird-feeding area in the snow, try snow painting with food coloring and water. Don't let the cold weather limit you—just bundle up to stay warm. Be as creative as you can to come up with unique ways to have fun in the snow.

What ultimate snow day activities did we do?

Advice we'd give to others about playing in the snow:

134

How often does it snow where we live?

Describe a family memory related to snow:

Our favorite things to do in the snow are _____.

DIG IN

snow day

Think about everyday activities you do in summer.
Make a long list of them, then imagine how you
could translate these to winter or snow. Do you like to
play tag? Try snow tag! How about having a cookout? Try having a snow cookout either with a grill
or by making a winter campfire. It might take a little
creative thinking, but that's half the fun.

Draw pictures of at least three of the snow activities you did today. Then write down your favorite thing about each activity, so you can always remember them.

44 Attract birds to your backyard by offering food, water, and shelter.

INSTEAD OF ALWAYS venturing out to find nature, sometimes it's easier to create a space for nature to come to you. Songbirds are one of the most diverse, friendly, and easy groups of wildlife to welcome into your backyard. You just need three basic things—food, water, and shelter. (Think bird feeders, a birdbath, and birdhouses.) Chances are there are dozens of birds that will love to visit your yard for food and water. There is a variety of birdseed available, but black oil sunflower seed will attract the most diverse kinds of birds. You can also experiment with fun foods like grape jelly for orioles or live mealworms for bluebirds and robins.

Research together the birds that live in your area and how to attract them to your backyard. Then your yard is ready for a bird makeover! Start by installing a feeder and birdhouse. If you lure in birds and make them feel comfortable, they might even raise babies in the spring, too!

Birds we want to see are _____.

What did we do to give our yard a bird makeover?

_____

Birds we saw within a week of our bird makeover:

_____

══════════════════ Sketch ══════════════════

A sketch of our bird makeover spot:

Birds we saw within a month:

Our favorite bird is the _____ because_____.

Write a funny bird story that happened in our yard:

DIG IN

You can find birds just about everywhere. Here are some
other popular places to look beyond your backyard:

- a pond or lake
- the edges of an open field
- the banks of a river
- the beach
- a bird-feeding station at a nature center
- a forest
- the desert

Examine the insects you find on a bug safari.

BUGS, including true bugs like cicadas, insects like grasshoppers, and other invertebrates like spiders, are some of nature's most intriguing, yet unappreciated, animals. They often go unnoticed because they're so small. But if you spend a few moments looking at the bugs in your backyard, you'll see that they can provide hours of entertainment. Watch a line of ants marching along and imagine where they're going. View a dragonfly cruising the edge of a pond or a meadow. Watch a butterfly land on a flower and observe as it sips nectar with its freakishly long tongue. A bug safari is a great way to slow down and enjoy a nature moment!

To fully appreciate insects, you need to examine them closely. You might be able to observe some bugs just by crouching down and getting really close to them, watching them crawl and move about in their natural environments. To get even closer, use a bug net to scoop up a few species and look at their body parts with a magnifying glass.

Check out a book on insects from the library. What are some of our favorite species? Draw them here:

What else did we see on our bug hunt?

Where did we find the most bugs?

Why do we think they liked it there?

Observe a bug for at least 10 minutes and document what it did:

Who found the most bugs?

DIG IN

You can use a jar with airholes punched in the lid to temporarily hold any insect. Try capturing fireflies right at dusk and studying them through the jar. What part of them lights up? You can capture other bugs this way as well. Just don't forget to release them after 5 or 10 minutes of observation so they can continue with their lives!

What was our favorite bug that we found? Describe it in detail or draw it here:

Retreat to a secret escape or sanctuary in nature.

NATURE should be soothing and peaceful. Does your family have a nature hideaway or a secret escape? What is a secret nature escape, anyway? It's a place you can visit where time just disappears. It's a safe place where everyone can go relax and reflect on nature. It can be just about anywhere. Perhaps it's a fort or tree house you have built, or maybe it's just a small plot of ground under a certain tree, but every family should have a secret hideout in nature they can enjoy together.

When you all are in this secret place together, lean back against a sturdy tree and see what you can see together. Your family might also use this time to catch up on their nature journaling or to work in their sketchbook. No matter where the secret escape is, it's a place just for you and your family.

Where is our family's secret escape?

Here is a sketch of our secret escape:

What do we do when we're there?

Our favorite part about the place is _____.

DIG IN

It's good to have a family place you can all go to spend time together, but it's also important to have a space where people can spend time on their own. Both adults and kids can use alone time! This place can be the same as your secret escape or it can be a whole new place, but make sure everyone has a chance to be there alone when they like.

Volunteer a few hours with a local nature organization.

MOST NATURE ORGANIZATIONS rely heavily on service from dedicated individuals and families, and you are never too young (or old!) to start your volunteering. Some organizations plan service days when a large number of volunteers come together to complete a task or project. Others need regularly scheduled volunteers throughout the year. Many volunteer tasks are also some of the most fun duties—like taking care of animals, helping at a special event, greeting people at the front desk, filling the bird feeders, and planting flowers. Volunteering is also a great way to teach children about responsibility and community service. To get started, just call up a nature organization in your area. They will have plenty of ideas to get you involved!

What type of volunteering do we want to do?

What good skills or ideas do we have that we think could help?

What organizations could we work with in the area?

After visiting _____
                    (name of local organization)

here's what we learned about what they do:

During our day of volunteering, here's what we did:

How will our help impact our community?

Here are some other groups we'd like to help in the future:

Our favorite part of volunteering was_____.

DIG IN

A little thank-you goes a long way to these organizations. Make a handmade card to let them know how much their organization means to you and mail it to them. They'll love it!

Scout a fishing hole, and tell a tall tale about what you caught.

JUST ABOUT ANY SPLASH of water has the potential to be a good place to go fishing. It just depends on what kind of fish you are trying to catch. Some species of fish (especially trout) like cool water, while others (including bass and catfish) thrive in warmer waters. Don't get too far ahead of yourself, though. Those can be some hard fish to catch!

Lots of people first learn to fish by catching panfish like bluegill, sunfish, and pumpkinseed. These are spunky fish (they're also spiky, so be careful taking them off the hook) that are easy to catch. All it takes is a fishing pole and reel, some line, some hooks, and some bait.

A good first step to fishing is to contact your state wildlife agency. They will have information about fishing locations in the area as well as information on seasons, license requirements (kids can often fish for free if the adult has a license), and other regulations. A bait shop is also a great place for information. They can sell you a dozen worms or other bait, and give you pointers on where to go.

Once you catch your fish, be sure to take a picture. Then let it go so someone else can catch it.

Where did we go fishing?

======================= Sketch =======================

What did we use for bait? Draw it here:

If we were a fish, what kind would we be?

Sketch three different kinds of fish:

Our favorite part of fishing is _____

because _____.

Part of the fun of fishing is telling a tall tale, or a fish tale, that exaggerates what you caught. Here's our fishing tale:

_____

DIG IN

After you've mastered worm fishing, it's time to move onto a lure. Lures require a different set of skills, like casting! Have someone teach you to cast, or find a video online that can get you started. Practice your cast lots of times. Then when you get the hang of it, take it to the water and try to catch a big one!

49 Camp outside in a tent with your family.

PERHAPS YOU'VE PITCHED a tent once or twice in your backyard. Now it's time to load up the car and try a new destination! Find a campground within a few hours from your home, ideally a place you've never been to before. Then pack up the tent, sleeping bags, food, and other camping supplies and hit the road. Being on a camping trip makes you feel rugged because the outdoors is all around you. You'll probably get a little dirty when you're surrounded by nature. While some campgrounds feel like mini-neighborhoods with playgrounds, grills, and other modern amenities, others are set in the wilderness.

Wherever you go, camping is a great way to leave your everyday world and routines behind for a while. It makes you appreciate some of the simple things in life, enjoy quality family time, and catch up around the campfire. Enjoy every minute!

Where we went camping:

Who went on our camping trip?

Did we cook our own meals? What did we eat?

What did we see in nature while camping?

DIG IN

Some campgrounds offer rental cabins and yurts. Are you wondering what a yurt is? It's a sturdy round tent first used by nomads in central Asia, but now you can find them all over the world. Some yurts are almost luxurious inside! Sleeping in cabins and yurts might not exactly be roughing it, but it's still a great way to experience nature and a slightly more comfortable way to go camping!

What we'd do differently next time when camping:

Our favorite part of camping was _____.

=========================== Sketch ===========================

What's your ultimate camping site? Draw it here. What else does it have besides a tent? Perhaps you'll have a hammock or a campfire area. Let your imagination be your guide!

Record a video about your favorite backyard moments.

IT'S SO EASY to record a video these days. Computers, cell phones, and cameras often have the ability to take digital video. Video has always been a fun way to remember special moments and preserve the memories.

To keep the recording process as simple as possible, have everyone write down their memory first—or at least parts of their memory—in this journal. You can keep it general, but it's also fun to remember something specific, too. For instance, your best memory of a special weekend or your favorite part of summer are both great stories to tell. Practice telling the stories to one another before you even hit the record button. Once you're ready, take turns describing your memories, looking directly into the camera. Don't worry if you mess up a little bit—just keep going.

This is a great rainy-day activity. You can also change the setting and scenery of your video by recording it in the backyard or a special outdoor place.

About what special event do we want to record a video?

What are we going to use to record our memories?

Write a little about the stories we're going to tell. (Use extra space!):

DIG IN

If you have a bunch of nature photos, gather them into a digital slideshow set to music. You can find lots of easy-to-use programs online for creating with digital photos. Then it's pretty simple to just put all the photos together and choose a song you like or one that makes you think of being outside. After you're done, you can burn the slideshow to a DVD to watch it on TV, or e-mail the slideshow link to family and friends who couldn't be there with you.

Where are we going to do our recording and why?

What's the next video we want to do?

Did something funny happen while we were working on the video?

=============== Sketch ===============

Did we have any bloopers? Write about or draw it here.

51 Plant a veggie garden—big, small, or any size at all.

IT DOESN'T MATTER if you have a full acre or just a square foot to dig into—go ahead and plant yourselves a vegetable garden this spring. If you are short on space, try selecting a favorite veggie or two. You can also look for "patio" varieties that tend to grow smaller or are perfect for containers. If you have a bit more room, start with things you know you like, but then challenge yourselves to plant something you are less familiar with, too.

Most garden centers will have a huge selection of seedlings, or starter plants. They are simple because you just have to transfer them into containers or your garden plot. Some plants can just as easily be grown from seeds.

Did you know you can even grow potatoes by planting an "eye" from one? Ask someone at the garden center for advice!

Where will we plant our garden?

We planted _____.

The most fun part of gardening is _____.

The most difficult part is _____.

DIG IN

Instead of planting just vegetables for you to eat, plant some food for wildlife, such as plants that provide seeds for birds. Sunflowers are one of the best plants to grow, and there are dozens of different sunflower varieties you can try. If you like to eat sunflower seeds yourself, try growing mammoth sunflowers. They will grow to more than 6 feet tall, and if the birds don't steal all the seeds, you can dig out a few for yourself.

One new thing we would like to grow
next year is ------------------------------.

Make three sketches of the plants as they grow up. First sketch the seeds or seed-lings, then again as the plants grow, and finally after they are fully developed.

Climb up a big hill or mountain—all the way to the top.

IT CAN BE HARD work hiking up a really big hill or a mountain, but it's worth the effort. You will feel a huge sense of accomplishment when you reach the top. Then you'll enjoy stunning views, and you might be able to see across the Earth for miles and miles.

If you're going to make the climb to the top, you'll need the right gear and supplies. Here are a few things to plan for:

- Wear comfortable shoes that have good, rugged soles and enough support for hiking.
- Dress in layers. You might get hot during the climb, but then when you stop hiking, the air might be cooler.
- Other supplies you'll want to take along include sunblock, sunglasses, snacks, water, and a camera so you can capture that gorgeous view for yourself.
- Start off with large hills you can climb in an hour or less. Then as your family gets better at climbing, explore larger hills. No matter what, you'll never get tired of that final view and sense of accomplishment!

Sketch the hill or mountain we climbed:

DIG IN

It's easy to follow the beaten path when you're hiking, and this is a good idea when you're trying to make it to the top. But when you have a little extra time, venture off the trail with your family and explore a bit more. Pay attention to any warning signs that may be posted before you do, and take care. You don't have to go too far right away. Just explore a little at a time and see what else you can find.

How long did it take us to climb?

What did it feel like to climb a mountain?

Things we noticed in nature while on our hike:

What did we do when we got to the top?

What mountain or hill do we want to scale next?

Events and Resources

SEEKING OUT MORE WAYS to get outside and fill your nature journal? Take a look at these great annual outdoor events. Which ones would you like to attend this year?

GREAT BACKYARD BIRD COUNT

www.birdsource.org/gbbc

Mid-February

An annual weekend of bird counting helps scientists research and study birds around the country. To participate, you simply watch birds in your backyard and submit the results online.

WORLD POETRY DAY

www.un.org/en/events/poetryday/

March 21

Let nature inspire you every year for World Poetry Day. The event supports all styles of poetry and celebrates poetry's tie to other arts.

LET'S G.O. (GET OUTSIDE)

www.childrenandnature.org/movement/letsgo/

April

Spearheaded by the Children and Nature Network, this monthlong initiative rallies intergenerational groups of people to play, serve, and celebrate with events throughout the month of April.

NATIONAL PARK WEEK

wwwww.nps.gov/npweek/

April

The National Park Service administers more than four hundred parks, natural areas, seashores, battlefields, historic homes, and archaeological sites including at least one in every state, and National Park Week celebrates them all.

EARTH DAY

www.earthday.org

April 22

On Earth Day a worldwide network of festivals and rallies builds support for environmental programs while rekindling public commitment and community activism for the planet.

NATIONAL ARBOR DAY

www.arborday.org
Last Friday in April

The first Arbor Day was in the late 1800s, when J. Sterling Morton had the idea of setting aside a day for planting trees in his home state of Nebraska. Today, events are held throughout the country. While tree planting is still a focus, many highlight more broadly the role trees play in our lives.

INTERNATIONAL MIGRATORY BIRD DAY

http://birdday.org
Second Saturday in May

With support from the Environment for the Americas, this is a collection of events and bird festivals taking place from Canada all the way to South America. Together they embrace birds and the connections between birds, habitat, and cultures.

NATIONAL PUBLIC GARDENS DAY

www.nationalpublicgardensday.org
Friday before Mother's Day (May)

Public Gardens Day celebrates public gardens while raising awareness of the role botanical gardens and arboretums play in promoting environmental stewardship, plant and water conservation, green spaces, and education. Many gardening organizations offer events and free admissions during the Public Gardens Day.

BACKYARD GAME OF THE YEAR

http://clifkidbackyardgame.com
Spring to Early Summer
This contest celebrates the creativity of childhood by inviting kids 6–12 years old to invent their own backyard games.

GREAT AMERICAN BACKYARD CAMPOUT

www.greatamericanbackyardcampout.org
June
Each year a Saturday in June is selected for the Great American Backyard Campout, part of the National Wildlife Federation's Be Out There campaign. It encourages folks to try camping, even if it is in their own backyard.

NATIONAL GET OUTDOORS DAY

www.nationalgetoutdoorsday.org
June
One Saturday in June, a coalition of nearly one hundred government, nonprofit, and outdoor recreation industry partners host events at almost two hundred locations. All events emphasize healthy, playful, outdoor fun and activities.

NATIONAL TRAILS DAY

www.americanhiking.org/national-trails-day/
Early June

The American Hiking Society celebrates trails all over the country by encouraging you to get outside and explore. Find an event near you or create your own.

FOURTH OF JULY BUTTERFLY COUNT

www.naba.org/butter_counts.html
July

The North American Butterfly Association oversees annual butterfly counts during the summer. Established counts help monitor butterfly populations, while raising public awareness and interest in butterflies. They are also tons of fun.

NATIONAL PUBLIC LANDS DAY

www.publiclandsday.org
September

With added emphasis on volunteering and stewardship, National Public Lands Day educates about the environment and natural resources by building partnerships with agencies and local communities. Roll up your sleeves and get involved.

NATIONAL WILDLIFE REFUGE WEEK

www.fws.gov/refuges/
Mid-October

Celebrate the more than 550 National Wildlife Refuges with Refuge Week held annually in October. National Wildlife Refuges are great to visit anytime during the year, but most offer special programming during this event.

PROJECT FEEDERWATCH

http://birds.cornell.edu/pfw/
November–April

Reporting the birds in your own backyard can contribute to science. Project FeederWatch is a winter-long survey of birds that visit backyards and nature centers throughout North America and is administered by the Cornell Lab of Ornithology and Bird Studies Canada.

CHRISTMAS BIRD COUNT

http://birds.audubon.org/christmas-bird-count
Late December–Early January

You can take part in the longest running citizen science project in the world. With numerous count circles in every state, there is bound to be one near you. New birders are paired up with experts, so everyone is encouraged to participate.

NOTES AND SKETCHES

Notes and Sketches

About the Authors

STACY TORNIO grew up growing vegetables, raising bees, and climbing trees in Oklahoma. Now she lives in Milwaukee, Wisconsin, where she loves exploring nature with her husband, Steve, and their two kids, Jack and Annabelle. She is the editor of *Birds & Blooms* magazine and the author of three other books.

KEN KEFFER grew up skipping rocks, riding his bike, and camping out in Wyoming with his younger brother. Now he is an environmental educator and author based in Milwaukee, Wisconsin. This is Ken and Stacy's second book together.

Visit Ken and Stacy online at destinationnature.net.

About the Illustrator

DENISE HOLMES is an illustrator and designer who lives in Chicago with her husband and daughter. When she is not in her studio drawing images of children, trees, and cats, she is out with her family exploring the city's parks, museums, and lakefront. You can visit her and read about her latest adventures at www.niseemade.com.